Original title:
Tropical Dreamscapes

Copyright © 2025 Creative Arts Management OÜ
All rights reserved.

Author: Matthew Whitaker
ISBN HARDBACK: 978-1-80581-597-6
ISBN PAPERBACK: 978-1-80581-124-4
ISBN EBOOK: 978-1-80581-597-6

Sands of Phantasia

On a beach where mermaids do laugh,
A crab wears a crown, what a gaffe!
Seagulls steal fries from my plate,
My sunburnt skin, fate tempts to wait.

Flip-flops stuck, I tumble down,
Bikini-clad dogs roam this town.
The sand's so hot, my feet scream loud,
Chasing the waves, I feel so proud.

Cascading Waterfalls

Waterfalls dance, they giggle and spin,
Fish wearing glasses think they're like kin.
With soap-filled bubbles floating near,
I slip and slide—oh, do I cheer!

A splash from a frog, he's quite the joker,
Wearing a hat, he looks like a smoker.
I wave to the ducks, they quack with flair,
At this waterfall, I shed all care.

Celestial Garden

In a garden where skies taste like pie,
Flowers sing songs, and kites fly high.
The bees wear suits, quite dapper they seem,
While clouds do nap, lost in a dream.

The carrots tap dance, they wiggle with glee,
While radishes tease, "Come play with me!"
A snail joins in with a modish hat,
"Oh, such fine friends, come grab a mat!"

Moonlit Hideaway

Under the moon, where starlight does glow,
A raccoon juggles, stealing the show!
The owls wear glasses, reading their scrolls,
While fireflies waltz, lighting up holes.

In this hideaway, all giggles and glee,
A fox DJs, with squirrels as the spree.
We dance till dawn, with no care to flee,
Moonlit mischief, wild and free!

Infinite Vistas

Palm trees sway, a dance with grace,
While flip-flops chase each other in place.
Seagulls gossip in the salty air,
And sunscreen battles with salty hair.

The sun's a joker, playing with rays,
While beachballs bounce in hilarious ways.
Children splash in a water fight,
As laughter echoes, pure delight.

Rhythms of Paradise

Coconuts drop with a comical thud,
While locals laugh, splashing in the bud.
Hula skirts twirl with awkward flair,
Creating a scene that's rare beyond compare.

A parrot squawks jokes from high above,
His vibrant feathers, a comedic glove.
Tiki torches flicker, casting quite the scene,
As dancing feet chase shadows pristine.

Kaleidoscope Shore

The sand is soft beneath my toes,
While sandcastles teeter, ready to doze.
Crabs in tuxedos scurry about,
With a pinch and a sprint, they're off in a rout.

Waves whisper secrets to seashells thronged,
As beachcombers hum their favorite song.
A splash from a wave, a shriek, then a grin,
As flip-flops soar, let the laughter begin!

Feathers and Fronds

In the jungle, vines twist and twine,
While monkeys laugh, sipping on sunshine.
A toucan sneezes, feathers in a flurry,
And all the parrots start to scurry.

Lizards sunbathe without a care,
While frogs croak choruses, loud and rare.
The leaves start dancing, joining the fun,
As nature giggles beneath the sun.

Serenities of the Coral Kingdom

In a sea of coral, fish wear hats,
Turtles enjoy tea with little chats.
Octopuses juggle with seaside flair,
While sea urchins giggle without a care.

Crabs do the cha-cha on sandy shores,
And dolphins play fetch with seaweedcores.
All join the party, a grand affair,
Underwater dancing, without a care.

Dreamseeds on Whispering Winds.

Kites made of laughter, floating so high,
Carried by wishes that paint the sky.
Clouds wear tutus, doing a jig,
While rain showers sprinkle, a boisterous gig.

Stars do a waltz with the moonlit sea,
Whispers of breezes call out with glee.
Balloons filled with dreams float, round and bright,
In this world of whimsy, all feels just right.

Emerald Horizons

Lush hills tickle toes with soft grass strokes,
Giggling mountains share their funny jokes.
A monkey wearing glasses reads the news,
While parrots gossip in colorful hues.

Sunsets burst forth with laughter and cheer,
As fireflies dance, drawing close and near.
Even the waves giggle as they roll,
In the emerald world that uplifts the soul.

Whispering Palms

Palm trees tell secrets with rustling leaves,
Swinging their branches as laughter weaves.
Coconuts chuckle, drop down for fun,
Playing hide-and-seek with the warm, bright sun.

The sand tickles toes, a soft, sweet tease,
As crabs scuttle away, protecting their keys.
In this verdant paradise, joy lifts the mood,
Where mirthful nature always seems good.

Serenity's Canvas

In a hammock strung between two trees,
Monkeys steal my snacks with ease.
The parrot laughs at my sunburned nose,
While I sip coconut milk and doze.

Palm leaves rustle like whispering friends,
As laughter and mischief never ends.
A crab scuttles by, wearing my flip-flop,
He takes it home, I just laugh and stop.

Sunlit Fantasies

Under bright umbrellas, we spread some cheer,
Chasing each other with frozen treats near.
A seagull swoops down, my ice cream's gone,
Now I'm left with just a half-eaten cone.

Sand castles rise, but they tumble and fall,
As kids yell, 'Look! Shells are perfect for all!'
But the dog thinks they're toys, what a scene,
He knocks them apart, the destruction is keen.

Chasing the Horizon

A surfboard waits, in the sparkling waves,
But I'm stuck in my towel, oh how it behaves!
My friend catches a fish, but it's really a shoe,
We both burst out laughing, what else can we do?

The sunset pours colors that paint the sky,
As crabs do a shuffle, oh my, oh my!
With beach balls flying, all round and bright,
The night ends in giggles, under moonlight's delight.

Fabled Shores

On the golden sands, I spot a rare shell,
But a seahorse swoops in and says, 'Do tell!'
It traded for tales of the ocean's grand lore,
While I just nod, stunned by its score.

A treasure map scribbled on a napkin found,
Leads us to giggles and silly sounds.
With weird-shaped fruit that's not at all sweet,
We feast on our laughter and dance to the beat.

Serene Shores

On the beach, a crab does moonwalk,
A clam shouts, "Hey! Don't block!"
Seagulls jesting in a silly spree,
While sunbathers scream, "Don't tan me!"

Sandcastles tumble like a bad joke,
Kids giggle as their dreams croak.
Waves crack up, their foamy lines,
Tickling toes, with wavy signs.

Lush Oasis

In the shade where the monkeys prance,
Bananas slip, they take a chance.
Parrots squawk, their gossip flows,
While frogs hop in ridiculous shows.

Palm trees dance in breezy flair,
Cacti laugh, spiking the air.
Lizards sunbathe with silly grins,
While sipping drinks that spin and spins.

Sunlit Canopy

Under blossoms, the bees conspire,
To tickle flowers with buzzing choir.
Squirrels chuckle, doing flips,
In a race with lazy, sleepy chips.

Sunbeams tickle all the leaves,
While shadows play with sunlit thieves.
A lizard dressed in shades so cool,
Struts his stuff like a glamorous fool.

Mirage of Colors

Rainbows sprout from paint-splashed skies,
While hippos try to dance with flies.
Turtles wear hats, they think it's fab,
Though they shuffle like a wobbly slab.

Giggling flowers bloom all around,
Tickling toes on the vibrant ground.
Clouds tumble in a cotton candy race,
As laughter echoes in this dream-like space.

Ribbons of Light

Balloons float high in silly shapes,
A parrot thinks he's wearing capes.
Sunshine tickles my funny bone,
While flip-flops dance on pavement stone.

Clouds are cotton candy spun,
Ice cream cones melt, oh what fun!
Laughter bubbles like a stream,
In this wild and wacky dream.

Echoes of the Tropics

Coconuts fall with a funny thud,
As I trip on a wayward bud.
Crabs do a jig along the shore,
While seashells giggle, wanting more.

A sea turtle gives a cheeky grin,
It seems to know where I've been.
With waves that whisper silly songs,
In this land where whimsy belongs.

Kaleidoscope Dreams

Colors burst like a clown's parade,
Palms sway with a rhythmic charade.
Why does the sun wear shades today?
It's a party that's here to stay!

Hammocks swing with a gentle sigh,
As birds dive down from the sky.
Sandcastles with silly flags unfurl,
In this jolly, sunlit swirl.

Warm Embrace of Sunlight

Under the rays where giggles bloom,
I see a lizard dance in the room.
Sunscreen slathers become a game,
While flip-flops grow tired of their fame.

An umbrella spins, a wild delight,
While seagulls gossip, birds in flight.
With every chuckle and silly grin,
Life's sweet laughter pulls us in.

Enchanted Islands

On an island where coconuts dance,
A parrot sings in a funny romance.
Sunburned tourists, quite out of sync,
Sip on their drinks—too much stinky pink!

Mermaids giggle at sunbathing whales,
Chasing after fish with oversized pails.
They trade fish tales for a shiny flip-flop,
While palm trees sway and the laughter won't stop.

A crab holds court with a crabby demeanor,
Trying to sell seashells as a wise schemer.
But tourists just laugh, saying, "What's that worth?"
As sand castles tumble, it's a messy rebirth!

So let's toast to the folly of sun-scarred bliss,
With fruity drinks served at a beachside kiss.
On these enchanted shores, life's a burst of fun,
Where every mishap becomes a pun under the sun!

Mysteries of the Bay

In the bay where the fish wear silly hats,
A dolphin debates with a pair of chatty rats.
Seagulls squawk in a comical crown,
For the best fish fry—they all come around!

A crab with a net tries to catch the tide,
But instead finds a boot from the local pride.
He claims it's a treasure fit for a king,
While the waves just snicker and continue to sing.

With jellyfish dancing in glittery skirts,
They throw a wild party, causing giggles and spurts.
All the fish join in with a flippery cheer,
"Let's dance till the tides even disappear!"

As the sunset spills colors across the bay,
Laughter and fun chase the troubles away.
So grab your snorkel and paddle along,
In the mysteries here, you can't go wrong!

Elysian Escapes in Green Light

In a jungle where turtles do cartwheels,
Laughter dances through banana peels.
Parrots squawk in a tune so absurd,
Even the palm trees can't help but be stirred.

Coconuts play hide and seek in the sand,
While monkeys juggle with all that they planned.
The sun wears sunglasses, oh what a sight,
In this giddy land, everything feels light.

Secrets in the Breath of the Wind

Whispers float by like a kite on a string,
A crab in the shell thinks he's the king.
The breeze tells jokes as it tickles my nose,
The flowers chuckle, and a rose garden grows.

A turtle tells tales with a grin ear to ear,
While the waves roll in, passing gossip and cheer.
I caught the wind giggling, oh what a tease,
As it sneaked past the palms with such agile ease.

Adrift in Colors of the Abyss

A fish in a hat swims around in a swirl,
While starfish debate who's the best at a twirl.
Octopuses juggle pearls like they're candy,
In the depths of the sea, they're all feeling dandy.

Corals hummed tunes that bubble and pop,
Sea cucumbers formed quite the fun flop.
With colors so vibrant, oh what a mess,
Underwater laughter, who needs to impress?

Sleepy Islands of the Rising Moon

On sleepy shores where dreams take a nap,
Crickets and clams join in for a clap.
The moon tells secrets to stars up above,
While the waves simply shrug, how they love!

A hammock swings low, tied to a tree,
Where a sloth stirs slowly, as happy as can be.
With pillows of clouds, and blankets of night,
These islands are cozy, wrapped up so tight.

Saltwater Symphony

Waves clap hands with sandy toes,
Seagulls serenade in silly prose.
Mermaids giggle while sipping tea,
Jellyfish dance like it's fancy free.

Sunglasses perched on a crab's small nose,
Starfish spot a fashion show in pose.
Coconuts roll like they've lost their mind,
Palm trees sway, oh, the laughs you'll find.

Radiant Reveries

Flip-flops flap like they're in a race,
Beach balls bounce, finding their place.
Lemons wear hats and dance with flair,
Tacos join in with a festive air.

Sunscreen soldiers line up on the deck,
A crab in shades gives a royal peck.
Lime slices giggle, zestfully bright,
As cocktails cheer with a splash and delight.

Prismatic Horizons

Kites fly high, a color parade,
Rainbows grin in the sun's warm shade.
A dolphin dives with a flip and spin,
While coconuts giggle, let the fun begin.

In the sandcastles, kings and queens reign,
With ice cream cones in a whimsical train.
Seashells chatter, gossiping too,
As flip-flops tango in the ocean's blue.

Glistening Auras

Hula hoops twirl like a whirlwind's jest,
While laughter bubbles, it's nature's fest.
Bananas giggle, slipping with glee,
As fish do the cha-cha, oh what a spree!

Palm trees whisper secrets to the breeze,
Feet in the sand, enjoying the tease.
A pelican's hat makes the gossip rise,
In this silly world, joy never dies.

Forgotten Paths through the Jungle

In the thicket where monkeys dance,
A toucan wears its pants askew.
Lizards sunbathe in a trance,
While parrots sing a tune so blue.

The vines twist like a cheeky grin,
With pesky bugs doing the cha-cha.
A sloth thinks it's winning a spin,
But naps away like it's a ballerina.

Rain drops down like silly confetti,
Splashing down on a clumsy gator.
Frogs leap with joy, feeling all petty,
While a turtle claims, "I'm the skater!"

Every path winds in playful jest,
Where laughter echoes through the trees.
In this jungle, life's a fest,
Chasing the breeze with cheeky ease.

The Call of the Sapphire Sea

Waves roll in with a giggle and flip,
As dolphins pull pranks in their spree.
Seashells wear hats in a light-hearted trip,
While crabs practice their tap dance for free.

The sun dives down like a playful kid,
Splashing colors on the bright blue stage.
Fish flash by, doing tricks they hid,
While octopuses write the next great page.

Beach balls bounce with no care in sight,
As seagulls steal fries from the sunbathers.
Sunburned folks turn a funny hue bright,
While waves whisper the tales of sailors.

In this sea where giggles don't end,
Each moment bursts with joyous play.
As tides change, we wade with a friend,
In the laughter of the ocean's ballet.

Inked Waves of an Infinite Sky

Clouds drift by in a haphazard swirl,
Like cotton candy lost its mind.
A paper airplane makes a twirl,
While birds try to outwit the wind, intertwined.

Kites dart through the limitless blue,
Tangled strings form a silly array.
A squirrel claims it flew too,
With that bluff, the wind just gave way.

Stars giggle from their glittering heights,
As a comet tries its hand at a dance.
Moonbeams laugh through the peaceful nights,
While dreams chase each other in a frantic prance.

In this sky where joy never fleets,
We sketch our thoughts in the sun's bright hue.
With whispers of wonder, the heart beats,
As the infinite dreams drift past, just a few.

Serenade of the Wild Waterfalls

Water tumbles with a raucous cheer,
While rocks act as stages for show.
Frogs croak prompts, oh so clear,
As fish join in for an aquatic go.

A bear joins in with a cheeky spin,
Dancing along to the splashy beat.
While a raccoon takes a goofy win,
Juggling fish with its paws—oh, what a feat!

Mist rises up, tickling the trees,
As the waterfall sings a sprightly tune.
Nature's laughter rides on the breeze,
Beneath the smiling gaze of the moon.

In this wild, the spirits play free,
Every drop brings a tale to tell.
With joy that flows like the gushing spree,
In a serenade where all souls swell.

Eden Dreams

In a garden where bananas wear hats,
An avocado sings as a cat chats.
Coconuts dance in a limbo spree,
While pineapples giggle up in the tree.

The sun spills juice on a hammock swing,
Where flamingos waltz, doing their thing.
Worms in tuxedos throw a grand ball,
Uninvited ants crash and trip, oh, what a fall!

Mangoes juggle with tumbling pears,
While coconuts paint creative flares.
In this paradise of quirky delight,
Every sunset is a comical sight.

So come join the party, there's plenty of fun,
With laughter and joy, under the sun.
For in this realm, wacky dreams weave,
And silly antics never take leave.

Wandering Through Paradise

Amidst crazy palm trees with wild fronds,
Lemonade rivers carry my bonds.
The lizards wear shades, all cool and sly,
While beetles play poker, oh my, oh my!

Baboons in skirts are knitting away,
As parrots perform a Broadway ballet.
Beach balls bounce off coconut walls,
With sea shells laughing, running down halls.

The waves tease penguins, oh what a sight,
Turtles wear sandals, feeling just right.
Every footstep is met with a cheer,
In this land of wonder, there's nothing to fear.

So let's roam around, in flip-flop blog,
With sand between toes, in this sunny fog.
With giggles and glee at every turn,
In this zany place, there's much to learn.

Radiance of Nature

Sunflowers giggle, with petals so bright,
While violets wear glasses, what a sight!
Butterflies prance, playing peek-a-boo,
And ants just can't get over their shoe.

Clouds play hide and seek with delight,
Ticklish raindrops sparkle in the light.
A squirrel tells stories of nuts he has seen,
To a captivated crowd of leafy green.

The trees spin tales of winds and storms,
While frogs in tuxedos create quirky forms.
Nature's a circus, each act a surprise,
Where laughter echoes beneath the blue skies.

In this vibrant scene, joy spreads so wide,
Even the rocks smile, it's hard to hide.
With each ray of sun, a chuckle we win,
In this radiant world, let the fun begin!

Joyful Horizons

The horizon laughs; what a silly view,
As the sun tries to put on its shoe.
Clouds tumble down like a fluffy brigade,
While rainbows giggle in brightly-bright parade.

Exotic fruits wear sparkly crowns,
As parrots crack jokes, stealing the crowns.
The oceans hold secrets beneath their blue,
And jellyfish twirl like they've lost their cue.

Dancing on waves, the dolphins play pranks,
With surfboards made of colorful flanks.
Every splash brings a giddy surprise,
While seagulls roll over, laughing with cries.

Let's leap with joy, on this playful expanse,
Where silliness sparkles, urging us to dance.
In this laughter-filled land, come take a peek,
For in joyful horizons, life's never meek.

Azure Whispers in the Canopy

In the jungle, a parrot sings,
With a voice that flaps its wings.
Monkeys swing on vines that break,
Shouting jokes that make us shake.

Bright frogs wear shoes made of glue,
Jumping high with a funny view.
Lizards dance in a conga line,
While iguanas sip on lime!

The sun smiles, casting a glow,
As palm trees sway in rows,
A toucan laughs, a loud "ha ha!"
In this world, we're all a star.

In shadows soft, the critters play,
With silly tricks, they steal the day.
Underneath the shade so bright,
Life's a carnival, pure delight!

Lush Horizons Beneath the Sun

Bright blooms dance in summer's breeze,
Sunshine tickles, making us sneeze.
Squirrels in sunglasses, looking cool,
Running around like they own the school.

Bumblebees buzz in a funky beat,
Wiggling between the flowers sweet.
A dancing crab has got some moves,
For a beach party, the sand approves!

Coconuts fall with a thud,
While we laugh and play in the mud.
A hermit crab rolls by with style,
Making everyone grin and smile.

Dolphins splash, they frolic and leap,
Their antics make us laugh and weep.
In this paradise, joy is clear,
A wild adventure, year after year!

Beneath the Swaying Palms

Under palms, the shadows blend,
With frisky lizards that twist and bend.
A chameleon changes in a flash,
Frog friends giggling in a splash!

Salty air brings tales galore,
As seashells whisper on the shore.
A crab with swagger walks the line,
With sunglasses perched—oh, how divine!

Hammocks sway, a sleepy dance,
While jays burst in—give life a chance!
Palm trees find their groove at night,
A concert under twinkling light.

The moon chuckles, painting the sea,
As fish tell secrets and swim carefree.
In this world, where laughter reigns,
The antics flow through joy's sweet veins!

Celestial Dolphins in Coral Seas

Above the waves, the sunbeams play,
While dolphins leap in a watery ballet.
They wear bright hats that float with ease,
Synchronized dance, they aim to please!

Coral reefs, a laughing stage,
Where fish pirouette—a colorful page.
A clownfish juggles shells in a swirl,
While starfish cheer, giving a twirl.

Seashells whisper on ocean's floor,
Telling tales of adventures galore.
A sea turtle rolls, with glee he spins,
In this underwater world, everyone wins!

As the sun dips low, the sky ignites,
With hues that blend on this fine night.
The dolphins giggle, they spin and glide,
In this cosmic sea, joy won't hide!

Celestial Cascades

In the jungle where monkeys play,
Fruits fall down like a buffet.
Lizards dance in their silly shoes,
While the parrots gossip the wildest news.

Coconuts roll like bowling balls,
Bamboo shoots are the funniest stalls.
Palm trees sway in a goofy jig,
While crabs compete in a silly gig.

Butterflies flutter with wacky flair,
Chasing each other without a care.
In this paradise of vibrant hues,
Laughter echoes with every muse.

Each wave sprinkles a splash of cheer,
As dolphins dance, they draw us near.
In the silliness of this grand tour,
Life's a beach, who could ask for more?

Waves of Serenity

Surfboards smile on the sandy shore,
Waves whisper secrets, always want more.
Seagulls squawk with a bit of sass,
Diving down for a chance to pass.

Turtles race in a slow-motion plot,
Each one hoping to win a lot.
The ocean's a playground, full of surprise,
As fish wear wigs and play dress-up guise.

Umbrellas twirl in the swirling breeze,
Ice cream melts, oh what a tease!
Sandcastles boast of grand designs,
While crabs critique their sandy confines.

With laughter bubbling like ocean foam,
We find mischief as we roam.
In this place where joy meets sun,
Every moment feels so fun!

Oasis of Light

Sunflowers giggle in the warm, bright rays,
Donkeys dance in amusing ways.
Cactus wears a silly hat,
While bees buzz tunes to the playful cat.

Watermelons roll like bowling spheres,
Laughing at our silly fears.
Palm fronds dance with a gentle sway,
While iguanas join the cabaret play.

In this hideaway of laughter and glee,
Every shadow hums a mystery.
Kites float high with a mission to tease,
While we sip coconuts with joyous ease.

The sun sets low, a orange delight,
As fireflies twinkle, bringing the night.
In this cheerful escape, spirits bloom,
With every laugh, we banish gloom.

Sunbeam Sanctuaries

Bubbles wander through fields of green,
Silly frogs leap, a comical scene.
Sunbeams sprinkle laughter on flowers bright,
Happiness blooms, a curious sight.

Hammocks swing with a gentle tease,
While ants march on, just to please.
The sun smiles down like a playful friend,
As nature giggles, the fun won't end.

Lemonade spills with a fruity splatter,
As children giggle, oh what a clatter!
With clouds like candy, floating above,
In this sanctuary of laughter, we love.

As night falls with its twinkling cheer,
Fireflies dance, drawing us near.
In this land of whimsy and light,
We laugh together, hearts feeling bright.

Celestial Flourish

A parrot wears a crown of fruit,
Sipping nectar, feeling cute.
Lizards dance in a funky way,
Belly shimmies in full play.

Beneath the sun, a monkey swings,
Pretending he's the king of things.
Coconut hats on every head,
While roaches keep a conga spread.

The iguana strikes a pose so grand,
With shades on, showing off his brand.
While fish gossip in the stream,
Plotting parties in a dream.

At dusk, hats fly up with glee,
As crabs host a jamboree.
Stars twinkle, and the night sways,
In this kingdom, joy obeys.

Luminescent Dreams

Fireflies wear tiny capes at night,
Their dance is pure, an awesome sight.
Snakes in shades do snake-y things,
While frogs don crowns and spread their wings.

The stars descend to join the fun,
Messy hair, a real home run.
Turtles toss a bamboo dice,
Shouting 'double!'—that's so nice.

Waves crash with a splashy cheer,
As dolphins roll; they persevere.
Lovable fish in fancy suits,
Participate in fruit disputes.

Through the night, we laugh and play,
In this wild and wacky way.
Every moment filled with gleam,
Living out the wildest dream.

Rhapsody of Colors

A flamingo paints with feet so bright,
Spinning circles, a flying kite.
Yellow parakeets share their tunes,
While turtles joke beneath the moons.

Little monkeys, so mischief-bound,
Swinging high without a sound.
Bees wear dresses made of lace,
Buzzing proudly, they set the pace.

The jungle's colors burst and sway,
As iguanas leap and play.
Peacock tails fan out so wide,
Flaunting hues with swagger and pride.

In this chaos, we shall dive,
With all these critters, we feel alive.
Laughter rings through the leafy lane,
As we dance in the tropical rain.

Echoes of the Wild

The parrots chatter, oh so loud,
As frogs croak deep, feeling proud.
Raccoons wear sunglasses all day,
While sloths nap close, dreaming away.

Lemurs serve banana splits on high,
Under palm trees, they wiggle and sigh.
Crabs do salsa on the shore,
With seashells clapping, asking for more.

Mangoes tumble in a fruity race,
While the sun covers them with grace.
Chameleons change to blend with glee,
In this paradise, wild and free.

As night falls, the moon declines,
To join the dance of twisty vines.
Here we swirl, as laughter echoes,
In the wild where joy bestows.

Sun-kissed Reveries Above the Waves

The sunbeams dance on a vibrant tide,
Seagulls gossip while crabs try to hide.
A fish in sunglasses flips like a pro,
"Catch me if you can!" it says with a glow.

Beach balls bounce like they're full of glee,
Flip-flops squeak like they're made to be free.
A pineapple hat on a beach bum's head,
He claims he's royalty, enough said!

Sandy toes wiggle, feeling quite grand,
Surfboards regale tales of the land.
A coconut laughs, clinking with glee,
As waves tell secrets, just you and me.

With laughter echoing under the sun,
Every splash and giggle, all part of the fun.
So come take a dip in this ocean of cheer,
Where the milkshakes flow and the world seems so clear!

Silhouette of a Caravan of Stars

Stars in a line march across the night,
Winking and blinking, what a sight!
A comet trips over its own little tail,
While meteors giggle, leaving a trail.

A milky way cruise with an alien crew,
Paddling in orbits, oh, who knew?
With cosmic donuts and sips of space tea,
They toast to the planets, just you and me.

Nebulas whisper jokes, swirling around,
Planets burst into laughter without making a sound.
"Earth's got the best memes!" a star boldly cries,
As constellations share stories under skies.

As night gets older, the giggles don't cease,
The playful stardust bursts like confetti of peace.
In this carnival of light, so bright and bizarre,
Dimples of laughter sparkle, our own little star!

Sips of Honeyed Air

In gardens where laughter blooms and spins,
Butterflies dance where the joy begins.
A bee with shades sips nectar with flair,
Buzzing sweet tunes in the honeyed air.

Flowers gossip about the bees and the breeze,
As whispers of petals sway with ease.
A ladybug prances, wearing a grin,
"Life's a picnic; come join in!"

With frolicking frogs playing in the stream,
And clouds overhead sharing a silly dream.
The air is thick with sweet-flavored fun,
Where the sun tickles you, everyone's on the run!

So sip on the laughter, let worries depart,
With honeyed air wrapping 'round each heart.
In this whimsical garden, we spread our cheer,
And dance with the breeze, our worries unclear.

Mirage of Laughter and Light

In a desert of giggles, the sun beams bright,
Sand dunes jive like they're losing the fight.
A mirage appears, wearing mismatched shoes,
"Join the dance party; you'll never lose!"

Cacti wear hats made of glittery dreams,
While tumbleweeds twirl like they're bursting at seams.
Squirrels in sunglasses roast marshmallows with care,
"Life's a campfire joke—come sit, if you dare!"

The horizon twists, stretching laughter so far,
As stars come out, each one a small star.
"Hide and seek?" whispers the moon in delight,
As the world gets fuzzy, bathed in the light.

In a mirage that sparkles with silly delight,
Forget to be serious, let joy take flight.
With giggles and chuckles, we find our own way,
In this land of laughter, we're bound to stay!

Where Hibiscus Paints the Day

Hibiscus blooms with a grin,
Sunshine spills from within,
Bees in hats buzz with cheer,
Whispering secrets, oh dear!

Palm trees sway in a dance,
Catch the breeze, take a chance,
Lemonade rivers flow by,
Swim with fish, oh my, oh my!

Silly monkeys wear shades,
Playing cards in cool glades,
Laughing loud, swinging high,
Underneath a marshmallow sky!

Nothing's serious here, just fun,
Floating clouds, sweet like icing bun,
Where the colors spin and twirl,
In this giggle-filled whirl!

Tides of Color in Paradise

Waves splash paint on the shore,
Colors giggle, want more!
Seashells dance to the beat,
Hiding treats in the heat.

Coconuts roll with a thud,
Acting silly, just like mud,
Starfish sing in the sun,
Making waves, oh what fun!

Lizards prance with a flair,
Wearing hats without a care,
Finding laughter in each tide,
Riding rainbows, side by side.

Castles built from dreams so high,
Where seagulls pinch a french fry,
In this land, joy's alive,
Dancing colors, oh we thrive!

Feathers of the Rainforest

Parrots chatter, what a tease,
Swinging on the vibrant trees,
Talking trees with leafy flair,
Joking with the jungle air.

Tiny frogs in tuxedos,
Waltzing through the verdant meadows,
In their tiny silly shoes,
They show off all of their moves!

Insects strut in bold attire,
Dancing flames of colors higher,
Twisting, turning, never shy,
Sipping nectar, oh my, oh my!

Rain drips down in a spoon,
While crickets hum a swoon,
Every leaf joins the fun,
Beneath the crazy green sun!

Dancing Shadows of the Coconut Grove

Coconuts play hide and seek,
Under leaves that sway and creak,
Shadows dance, a sly parade,
Every move is a new charade.

Lizards laugh with a twist,
Belly flops are not to be missed,
While crabs stumble in the sand,
Joining in a merry band.

Sunsets splash in shades of glee,
As fireflies twinkle, oh wee!
Moonbeams join the midnight waltz,
Holding hands, never a fault.

Underneath the coconut sway,
Where silly games replay,
Mirth explodes, cheers ignite,
In this grove, all is bright!

Velvet Sunsets

The sky drips gold atop the bay,
Where seagulls strut in a cheeky play.
Palm trees dance with silly grins,
As flip-flops fly and laughter spins.

A parrot's squawk, a coconut drop,
Mixing drinks with a funny hop.
In hues of pink, the night unfolds,
While beach cats argue over gold.

Tanned tourists in a merry fight,
With sunscreen battles that feel so right.
Hats blown off by a salty gust,
In this wild world, we just must trust.

So toast with laughs, let worries fade,
As sunset whispers, the twilight parade.
With each bright hue, our spirits soar,
In velvet sunsets, who could ask for more?

Waves of Enchantment

Frothy waves that tease the toes,
A crab scuttles, striking a pose.
Surfboards dance like birthday cakes,
As dolphins join in, doing high stakes.

A beach ball flies, lands on a head,
While seagulls snicker, 'Oh, look—he's fed!'
Sandy toes, a sculptor's delight,
Creating castles that lose their height.

Sun-kissed folks with silly hats,
Try to dance with random cats.
Ice cream cones drip like melted dreams,
In a world bursting at the seams.

Jellyfish umbrellas in the sky,
While future sunburns wait to lie.
With every wave, a chuckle or two,
Our joy is endless, like the ocean's blue.

Island Reverie

On this isle where dreams take flight,
A monkey steals a drink at night.
With ukuleles strumming with flair,
And flamingos posing without a care.

A hammock swings, a prize to win,
While tourists giggle and chug their gin.
Laughter bubbles in the ocean spray,
As sunset parties come out to play.

Turtles in shades strike a cool pose,
While mermaids giggle in nobody knows.
A treasure hunt for the lost seashell,
Spinning tales of the ocean's spell.

Barbecue dreams and the moon's soft gaze,
We dance 'til dawn in a happy daze.
Island life, a comical spree,
Where even a crab can be king, you see!

Celestial Coastlines

Stars wink down on the sandy shore,
As fish pull pranks, wanting more.
The moon's a beach ball in the sky,
While starfish giggle and glow on high.

Surfboards leap in cosmic play,
And jellyfish journey through a bright ballet.
With every splash, a joke unfolds,
As laughter rings in the night so bold.

Light-up drinks and silly hats galore,
A parade of clowns from the ocean floor.
Bubbles rise like wishes set free,
In this coastline lore, we find the key.

So gather 'round for a cosmic toast,
To laughter, dreams, and friends we boast.
In celestial arcs of fun and cheer,
We embrace the night, with smiles sincere!

Harmonies of the Breeze

Palm trees sway like silly dancers,
As I chase them with my funny prancers.
The coconuts fall with a thud,
Laughing at me as I slip in the mud.

Seagulls squawk, trying to rap,
While crabs backstage are taking a nap.
A breeze tickles my nose with glee,
I think it's flirting; it giggles at me.

Bikini tops must wear seatbelts,
To dodge the winds and avoid sudden meltdowns.
I'm tangled in tales spun by the sea,
Where even the sun wears shades just for me.

Flip-flops marching in a silly parade,
With a side of sunscreen, just to invade.
As dolphins chuckle at my beach bum dance,
I join in laughter; oh, what a chance!

Coral Reflections

Corals giggle in shades of pink,
As fishes gossip; they barely think.
I wear my goggles, ready for fun,
But end up tangled; oh, what a run!

The starfish wave with awkward grace,
While crabs make faces, a goofy race.
Rainbow shells hide secrets unfound,
I tripped on a seaweed; oh, what a sound!

The octopus juggles shells with flair,
While I attempt a flip—oh dear! Beware!
In this underwater circus, we float and soar,
Tickling sea monsters and begging for more.

Laughter bubbles beneath the waves,
With fishy jokes and generous braves.
As tides pull me into a whirlpool spree,
I'm the clownfish captain—so wild and free!

Adventurous Breezes

Kites are flying crazy high,
Chasing clouds like they're cake in the sky.
Ice cream spills down my sunny shirt,
While gusts of wind playfully flirt.

I rode a bike that's lost its chain,
Pedaling backwards, now isn't that plain?
Breezy whispers tickle my ear,
Suggesting I dance, oh what a cheer!

Lizards on logs wear tiny hats,
They wave their tails like theatrical brats.
Cocktails of fruit, a wild splash party,
With parrots that sing bold and hearty.

My flip-flops squeak as they laugh in dread,
Chasing me down the path I just fled.
Yet here I am, with both feet on sand,
Where laughter's free, and dreams are grand!

Magenta Mornings

Morning breaks in shades of fun,
As I trip over slippers, oh what a run!
Magenta skies drop sunshine hues,
While I negotiate with the morning snooze.

Birds chirp rumors of last night's feast,
Where crabs held court, and the seaweed ceased.
I pour my coffee into a shell,
While it splashes me back; oh, what a swell!

The hammock's tangled in laughter's breeze,
Swinging like a fish that forgot its keys.
Orange juice drips, making tiny streams,
It's a ballet of breakfast, a dance of dreams.

As the sun rises, I crack my grin,
With a cheeky wave to the waves that spin.
In this playful morning, so absurd and bright,
I embrace the chaos; oh, what a delight!

Secret Gardens of the Monsoon

In the garden, frogs wear hats,
Dancing on the lily pads.
It's a party, can you see?
Bumblebees serve cups of tea.

Mice are munching on the leaves,
While the gophers play with bees.
Rain comes down in sprightly jumps,
Making puddles for the chumps.

Tulips twirl in raincoat suits,
Chasing bugs in rainy boots.
Monsoon laughs, the sky's a tease,
As umbrellas sail like bees.

So let's prance through this delight,
Socks all soggy, that's alright!
In this madcap, sunlit spree,
Every drop's a joy, you'll see!

Velvet Skies and Mango Nights

Underneath a velvet spread,
Mangoes dance upon your head.
Stars like sprinkles, cheeky bright,
Whisper secrets into night.

Coconuts are plotting schemes,
Riding waves on wobbly dreams.
A parrot cracks a corny joke,
Laughter echoes as he croaks.

Mango chutney on the breeze,
Sweet and sour, if you please.
Joyful hiccups fill the air,
As the moon does jig and flare.

Every twinkle's full of glee,
Waves of laughter, wild and free.
In this land of fruits and fun,
A night like this can't be outdone!

Lullabies from the Island Shore

On the shore, the crabs sing low,
Twirling tales of tides and flow.
Seashells whisper soft and sweet,
While the fish tap dance and greet.

Coconuts in lullaby tones,
Rock the sand with sleepy drones.
Snoring waves, they tease and play,
Making sure we dream away.

A hammock strung between two trees,
Breezy naps and sandy knees.
Where the stars are twinkling bright,
Dancing shadows kiss the night.

So let's sway in sea's embrace,
Waves serenade this special space.
Laughter mingles with the tide,
A cozy, sleepy joy inside.

Echoes of a Sunset Breeze

As the sun begins to drop,
Seagulls circle, holler, hop.
Orange skies in funny shapes,
Waves clap hands like silly apes.

Sandy toes and giggles flow,
Watch the sunset put on a show.
The breeze plays tricks on our hats,
Making everyone look like brats.

Dancing shadows chase the light,
Crabs in tuxedos feel just right.
The echo of a joyful squeal,
Bounces between sunset meals.

We're all part of nature's jest,
Playing hard, enjoying rest.
In this place where fun's a breeze,
Every sunset brings us peace.

Serendipity by the Sea

Waves crash down with a silly shout,
Seagulls squawk like they're in a drought.
A crab dances sideways, what a sight!
While sunburned tourists wear socks at night.

Sandcastles melting, oh what a mess,
With moats that resemble a muddy dress.
Umbrellas wobble, tipped by the breeze,
While kids chase after a runaway sneeze.

Splashing about in a squishy pit,
While fish judge us, saying, 'Where's the wit?'
Shells like treasures, oh what a find,
But watch your step! A sharp one's not kind.

Ice cream drips while laughter erupts,
Chasing after joy, who really interrupts?
Boys dressed as pirates, girls play along,
Costa del Chaos, we all sing a song.

Blossoms at Dusk

Petals flutter like a silly dance,
As bees buzz round with a goofy prance.
Even the trees seem to sway with glee,
Though squirrels argue, 'That nut's for me!'

Sunset colors spill like melted hue,
While fireflies argue over who flew.
Laughter echoes in the cool evening light,
While owls look on, thinking, 'Is this right?'

Dancing shadows play hide and seek,
As frogs croak loudly, no need to be meek.
A breeze whispers jokes that only it knows,
While crickets sing songs of forgotten woes.

Overhead the stars begin to show,
A raccoon rolls in the flowers below.
With giggles echoing through the night air,
Even the moon wonders, 'Why such flair?'

Breezes of Promise

The wind wraps around like a cheeky friend,
Whistling secrets that sometimes offend.
Palm trees sway, playing peek-a-boo,
While coconuts chuckle, 'What's wrong with you?'

Kites soar high, catch a gust of cheer,
While beach balls bounce, "Hey, watch me here!"
Flip-flops flop, a cacophony grand,
As laughter bubbles, tickling the sand.

Salty snacks tease from beachside stalls,
"Did you say chocolate?" a seagull calls.
Kids with their buckets dig down for gold,
While parents roll eyes at the stories retold.

The sun sets down, a comical sight,
As the sand finally cools, transitioning light.
Stars peek out, giggling from above,
While nature unravels its crazy love.

Nature's Spell

The woods whisper secrets in playful tones,
As mushrooms giggle on their tiny thrones.
A squirrel does ballet on a crooked limb,
While rabbits applaud, 'Look at him swim!'

Leaves chuckle softly, rustling their tales,
While ladybugs race like they have tiny sails.
Even the brook sings a bubbly tune,
Inviting raccoons for a midnight swoon.

Sunbeams scatter, playing hide-and-seek,
While the fox, all in red, struts like a freak.
In shadows of trees, the owls conspire,
Chorusing mischief, lifting spirits higher.

With dusk settling in, the giggling won't end,
Nature's own party, what a delightful blend!
From cheeky to whimsical, it knows no bound,
In this forest of laughter, joy can be found.

Serenity Among the Waves

A lobster wearing shades, so bright,
He sips a drink, what a sight!
The crab in shorts starts to dance,
While seagulls plot their next romance.

Fish in tuxedos swim with flair,
While turtles gossip, unaware.
The waves giggle, tickle the shore,
As the sun shines on, begging for more.

Jellyfish fashion, oh so chic,
In flip-flops they stroll, so unique.
A dolphin dives, but then slips back,
In this party where nothing lacks.

The sandcastles wave their flags high,
As hermit crabs race, oh my, oh my!
Laughter bubbles in the salty breeze,
In this paradise, all hearts feel pleased.

Dancing Under Coconut Skies

Coconuts roll, with a funny sound,
As monkeys swing and spin around.
A pineapple wears a sparkly hat,
As palm trees sway in a dance so flat.

Beneath the sun, a limbo line,
With parrots squawking, "This is fine!"
A conga line of folks and cheer,
The night brings laughter, oh so dear.

With beach balls bouncing everywhere,
And laughter twirling through the air,
The crabs lead a conga parade,
While clams clap shells, a grand charade.

Under coconut skies, what a blast,
Where every moment flies by fast.
We twirl, we whirl, we sing and shout,
In this silly world, without a doubt.

Garden of Delights

In a garden where fruits giggle together,
A watermelon wears a lovely feather.
Bananas swing and share their laughs,
While peppers dance in little halves.

Tomatoes gossip about the weather,
Carrots form a rock band, oh what a tether!
A cabbage laughs at the turnip's face,
As daisies join in the merry chase.

Bees wear sunglasses, sipping tea,
While butterflies flutter, wild and free.
At sunset, the garden bursts with cheer,
With sights and sounds all drawing near.

From fruits to flowers, all unite,
In this garden, pure delight.
With silly stories shared each night,
We find our joy in moonlit light.

Tranquil Tides

Waves whisper secrets to the sand,
As starfish wiggle, feeling grand.
A seahorse in glasses, so refined,
Reads a shell book, one of a kind.

The clams hold court, with pearls to show,
While octopuses juggle in a row.
Anemones sway with gentle pride,
In this calm world, where joys collide.

Crabs in tuxedos sipping slush,
As dolphins dive, creating a hush.
The tide pulls back, then flows anew,
A merry dance, both old and true.

With every splash and joyful cheer,
The ocean's song is always near.
We laugh, we play, and let time flow,
In the peaceful tides that endlessly glow.

Mirthful Tides

In flip-flops they prance, quite out of sync,
Chasing crabs that dart, they squeal and wink.
A beachball escapes, like a runaway pet,
Laughter erupts, it's the best day yet.

Seagulls squawk loudly, stealing their lunch,
While sunscreen's smeared in a comical bunch.
They dance in the waves with a vibrant flair,
Water splashes high, and the sun's in their hair.

With each passing wave, another joke flies,
Belly laughs ringing beneath sunny skies.
Their hair's all a mess, but who even cares?
Amidst silly faces and joyous affairs.

The sandcastles topple, yet spirits stay bright,
As they try to surf, but just end up in flight.
With shenanigans rife under sun's golden shine,
These mirthful tides flow, oh how they align!

Ruby Skies

The sunset's a canvas, painted in cheer,
With splashes of crimson, a sight to endear.
They gallivant freely, shoes tossed aside,
While giggles erupt from the ocean's wide tide.

A pirate hat perched on a friend's crazy head,
They pretend to plunder, but just find bread.
Mermaids just giggle, their scales all aglow,
As these landlubbers seek treasures below.

With jokes flying high, like kites in the air,
They trip over roots, unaware of the scare.
Belly laughs echo as they run from a wave,
Squealing like seagulls, oh the joy they crave!

As the sun starts to dip, they form a conga line,
Moving in rhythm, it's a sight so divine.
With ruby skies glowing, their fun never dies,
In this playful paradise, where laughter just flies.

Wandering Whispers

Amidst palm trees swaying, a whisper takes flight,
It rustles the leaves, bringing giggles at night.
The shadows dance wildly, playing hide-and-seek,
With tones of mischief, laughter's what they seek.

A coconut falls, with a thud and a grin,
Landing precisely on a kin's silly chin.
The chats turn to chuckles, spinning tales of the past,
While the stars pop out like confetti so fast.

A chameleon winks, it changes its hue,
While these wandering souls just don't have a clue.
They stumble through giggles, with pranks here and there,

Taking turns tripping on sunshine and air.

With each whisper turning to raucous guffaws,
These revelations lead to absurd little flaws.
Under starlit embraces, they dream with delight,
Wandering whispers weave magic each night.

Embrace of the Isles

In an embrace of the isles, where time takes a break,
They juggle with pineapples, oh what a mistake!
The fruit goes flying, a slippery spree,
As laughter erupts and rolls in like the sea.

Sipping on coconuts, they share all their dreams,
But one friend's had too many; it bursts at the seams.
The milk flies like confetti, a joyous parade,
Leaving behind giggles and a coconut haze.

Underneath thatched roofs, the fun never ends,
With fables of fish that have far too many fins.
They birth local legends of the silly sea hare,
Each twist of the story incites quite a flare.

In this embrace of the isles, mischief is key,
As they caper and tumble, in pure jubilee.
With each crack of a joke, the sun starts to rise,
In this joyful embrace, where laughter defies.

A Symphony of Ocean Serenades

Waves are dancing, what a sight,
Seagulls squawking, taking flight.
Shells are laughing on the sand,
Crabs in tuxedos, oh so grand!

A dolphin sings, a fish taps toes,
Octopus drumming with all it knows.
Splashing tunes in watery glee,
Mermaids join the jamboree!

Sandcastles wear crowns of seaweed,
Shellfish strut, it's quite the breed!
Sunsets paint in colors bright,
Twirling joy in the glowing light.

Coconuts drop, they roll with flair,
Those lazy lizards lounging there.
Laughter echoes, nature's cheer,
Life's a party, let's draw near!

Mystical Ruins in Emerald Haze

In lush jungles, secrets sleep,
Ancient stones their promises keep.
Parrots gossip, mossy tales,
While monkeys giggle, swinging trails.

Palm trees peek through fragrant vines,
Whispering secrets, sipping wines.
Forgotten temples, look so bold,
They still dance in stories told!

Lizards hold court in the sun,
Claiming thrones, it's all in fun.
Breezes carry giggles in air,
As wild creatures stop and stare.

Echoes of laughter, moonlit night,
Ghosts of parties held in fright.
Here in hazes, life's a jest,
Adventure calls, come be our guest!

The Island's Heartbeat at Dawn

Sunrise tickles the sleepy skies,
Coconuts yawn with sleepy eyes.
Roosters crowing, quite the sound,
Bananas blushing, hanging round.

Smoothie makers, blending cheer,
Sipping fruit, it's finally here!
Waves are racing to touch the shore,
Tickling toes, always wanting more.

Seashells stash secrets from the night,
While crickets sigh in morning light.
Bamboo flutes play playful tunes,
As fishermen launch their afternoon.

Fish are swimming with a wink,
Painting patterns in the drink.
Life's a hoot in every hue,
On this island, dreams come true!

Nectar of the Moonlit Shore

Under stars, the coconuts sway,
Shells gleam bright on sandy bays.
A crab moonwalks, stealing scenes,
While fish flaunt their shiny sheens.

Whispers of waves, a lullaby,
As fireflies start to fly high.
Mangoes giggle, ripe with glee,
Pineapples join, dancing free!

Tiki torches nod in delight,
Charmed by shadows, soft and light.
The night's as sweet as honey's kiss,
In this haven, it's pure bliss!

Laughter bubbles under the moon,
Sea turtles slide, grooving to a tune.
Waves and whispers, a shared embrace,
In this realm, we find our place!

Exotic Echoes

In a land where the coconuts dance,
Parrots squawk in a silly romance.
Lizards wear shades with a snazzy flair,
While the sloths are just lounging without a care.

The palm trees sway to a bouncy beat,
Crabs tap their claws, oh what a feat!
A pineapple hat on a guy named Stu,
Claims he's the king of the fruit parade crew.

Monkeys juggle bananas, oh what a sight,
The iguanas are grooving all through the night.
A toucan shouts, "Let's have some fun!"
But they all get distracted by the setting sun.

With jellyfish bobbing in a bright hue,
The water's so warm, it's like a tea brew.
As waves crash and giggles fill the air,
Even the fish have a flair for the rare.

Horizon's Embrace

Under a sky painted bright and blue,
A crab wears flip-flops that he bought at the zoo.
Turtles in sunglasses drive scooters around,
While the dolphins are playing, doing flips off the ground.

The sunset's a disco, a vibrant display,
With flamingos dancing in their feathery sway.
A parakeet DJ spins tunes on the shore,
As the waves break and tumble, begging for more.

A beach ball rolls past a sunken treasure,
While seagulls squabble, oh what a measure!
The breeze carries laughter, it's quite a delight,
As coconut drinks keep the mood feeling bright.

Under the stars, they all gather 'round,
Sharing their tales with a giggly sound.
"Oh, catch that wave!" a voice suddenly shouts,
But it turns out to be just a crab with doubts.

Fragrant Currents

In the jungle where the mango trees sway,
A monkey steals snacks in a cheeky display.
Flavors burst forth like fireworks bright,
While honeybees hum tunes that feel just right.

Coconuts giggle as they drop from the palm,
The pineapple stands, looking fresh and calm.
A dragonfruit dreams of being the star,
While a coconut harps on its old guitar.

The sweet scent of blossoms fills the warm air,
As a lizard winks, with a grand flair.
A fruit salad party, all dressed up fine,
With dancing bananas, now that's divine!

Giggling gusts carry laughter around,
As the whole jungle joins in the sound.
"Tastes like sunshine!" a young bear declares,
As they all munch on treats without any cares.

Starlit Lagoon

By the moonlight, the waves shimmer and flow,
As turtles in tuxedos put on quite a show.
The frogs croak ballads, serenading the night,
While fishes tap dance, oh what a sight!

Fireflies twinkle like stars on the shore,
While a crab tells tales of days before.
"Oh, my shell is so heavy!" he sighs in jest,
"The ocean's a blast, but I need a rest!"

The jellyfish float by in a fanciful dance,
Inviting the lonely to join in the prance.
"Don't be shy!" says a clam with a wink,
"Join our conga, you just need to think!"

As night deepens, the laughter just grows,
The lagoon transforms into a stage of shows.
With giggles and splashes, the merriment swirls,
Under the stars, the lagoon joyfully twirls.

www.ingramcontent.com/pod-product-compliance
Lightning Source LLC
Chambersburg PA
CBHW072218070526
44585CB00015B/1395